D0615374

A Perspective on the Changing Business and Financial Environment

THE JOSEPH I. LUBIN MEMORIAL LECTURES

NUMBER 5

John J. Phelan, Jr.

Chairman and Chief Executive Officer
New York Stock Exchange, Inc.

A Perspective on the Changing Business and Financial Environment

The Joseph I. Lubin Memorial Lectures
Leonard N. Stern School of Business
Undergraduate College
New York University

NEW YORK UNIVERSITY PRESS
NEW YORK AND LONDON
1989

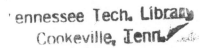

'ennessee Tech. Library
Cookeville, Tenn.

Copyright © 1989 by New York University
All rights reserved
Manufactured in the United States of America

Library of Congress Cataloging-in-Publication Data
Phelan, John J., 1931–
  A perspective on the changing business and financial environment /
John J. Phelan, Jr.
      p.   cm.—(The Joseph I. Lubin memorial lectures : no. 5)
  Lecture delivered at the Undergraduate College of the Stern School, New
York University, Mar. 1988.
  ISBN 0-8147-6608-0
  1. Securities industry—United States.   2. Finance—United States.
3. United States—Economic policy—1981–   I. Title.   II. Series.
HG4910.P46   1989   88-26829
332.64'0973—dc19   CIP

This lecture is dedicated to my father, John J. Phelan, who spent his entire professional life in the securities industry, was my teacher and mentor, and to whom I am forever indebted.

FOREWORD

The Joseph I. Lubin Memorial Lectures were established through the generosity of the late Joseph I. Lubin—a distinguished business, civic, and philanthropic leader and a trustee of New York University. This is the fifth of the Lubin Lecture series. These lectures are modeled after the college's past distinguished Moskowitz Lectures. The combined Lubin/Moskowitz Lecture series has been presented annually by the college for over 25 years. It has featured prominent business and academic leaders discussing the critical management, financial, and economic issues of our day. This year is certainly no exception, although when we arranged for Mr.

Phelan to speak in September of 1987 we had no inside information on the forthcoming stock market crash of October 19, 1987.

John J. Phelan, Jr., began his securities industry career with Nash and Company in 1955, becoming a partner in 1957. He was named managing director of its successor firm, Phelan & Company, in 1962. Following a second reorganization in 1972, he became a senior partner of Phelan, Silver, Vesce, Barry and Company. From 1959 to 1980, he was an active participant on the New York Stock Exchange's trading floor.

He was elected to the NYSE board of governors in 1971 and to the reorganized corporate-style board in 1974. In 1975 he was elected vice-chairman of the board, serving in that capacity until 1980 when he assumed the office of president and chief operating officer of the NYSE. In May of 1984 he was elected to his present position as chairman and chief executive officer of the New York Stock Exchange.

Under Mr. Phelan's leadership, the NYSE has been established as the world's premier securities marketplace. He has been a leader in calling for a worldwide effort to develop a global framework to ensure a competitive, orderly, and properly regulated worldwide securities market. He is widely credited with bringing the NYSE into the electronics age.

Mr. Phelan is no stranger to the university scene. Education has long been one of his major interests. He is a graduate of Adelphi University, he is past chairman of and is now trustee emeritus of the board of trustees of Adelphi University. In addition, he serves as a member of the board of trustees of Tulane University and the New York Medical College. He holds honorary Doctor of Law degrees from Notre Dame, Hamilton College, and Niagara University.

In addition to his educational activities, he is active in community and civic affairs. Mr. Phelan has twice served as Wall Street division chairman of the National Conference of Christians and Jews and is a recipient of the Brotherhood Award. He is a member of the New York Archdiocese Cardinal's Committee of Laity and the financial council of the Archdiocese. He serves on the board of trustees of Catholic Charities. He is also active with many other organizations including the Asia Society, the Boy Scouts, the Heart Fund, and the United Way. Mr. Phelan currently is a member of the board of directors of Eastman Kodak Company and of the Metropolitan Life Insurance Company.

I am grateful to my associate, Amanda Sherman, for her help in handling the details of arranging this year's Lubin lecture and the publication of this book.

May 24, 1988   DANIEL E. DIAMOND
                  Dean, Stern School of Business
                  Undergraduate College

The Joseph I. Lubin Memorial Lectures

The Joseph I. Lubin Memorial Lectures were established through the generosity of a distinguished trustee of New York University, the late Joseph I. Lubin. Mr. Lubin, who was a preeminent force in the business and philanthropic community, wished to provide a public forum for the discussion and practical application of economic and management theories.

This extraordinary humanitarian will also be remembered for his civic and philanthropic endeavors. He has enriched this city not only by New York University's Eisner & Lubin Auditorium, but also by his contributions of the Joseph I. Lubin Pace Schools of Business, the Joseph I. Lubin Syracuse House, and the Evelyn J. and Joseph I. Lubin Rehabilitation Center and Center for Learning Disabilities at the Albert Einstein College of Medicine. Mr. Lubin was a Gallatin Fellow and a Haskins Associate of the College of Business & Public Administration, New York University. He also served as a trustee of Syracuse and Pace Universities and of the Albert Einstein College of Medicine.

This volume is the fifth in the Joseph I. Lubin Memorial Lecture series and is modeled after our past distinguished Charles C. Moskowitz Memorial Lectures series. A complete listing of these lectures can be found on the following pages.

November, 1963   *The Common Market: Friend or Competitor?*
Jesse W. Markham, Professor of Economics, Princeton University
Charles E. Fiero, Vice President, The Chase Manhattan Bank
Howard S. Piquet, Senior Specialist in International Economics, Legislative Reference Service, The Library of Congress

November, 1964   *The Forces Influencing the American Economy*
Jules Backman, Research Professor of Economics, New York University
Martin R. Gainsbrugh, Chief Economist and Vice President, National Industrial Conference Board

November, 1965   *The American Market of the Future*

Arno H. Johnson, Vice President and Senior Economist, J. Walter Thompson Company

Gilbert E. Jones, President, IBM World Trade Corporation

Darrell B. Lucas, Professor of Marketing and Chairman of the Department, New York University

November, 1966   *Government Wage-Price Guideposts in the American Economy*

George Meany, President, American Federation of Labor and Congress of Industrial Organizations

Roger M. Blough, Chairman of the Board and Chief Executive Officer, United States Steel Corporation

Neil H. Jacoby, Dean, Graduate School of Business

Administration, University of California at Los Angeles

November, 1967   *The Defense Sector in the American Economy*
Jacob J. Javits, United States Senator, New York
Charles J. Hitch, President, University of California
Arthur F. Burns, Chairman, Federal Reserve Board

November, 1968   *The Urban Environment: How It Can be Improved*
William E. Zisch, Vice-Chairman of the Board, Aerojet-General Corporation
Paul H. Douglas, Chairman, National Commission on Urban Problems
Professor of Economics, New School for Social Research

17

Robert C. Weaver, President, Bernard M. Baruch College of the City University of New York
Former Secretary of Housing and Urban Development

November, 1969   *Inflation: The Problem It Creates and the Policies It Requires*
Arthur M. Okun, Senior Fellow, The Brookings Institution
Henry H. Fowler, General Partner, Goldman, Sachs & Co.
Milton Gilbert, Economic Adviser, Bank for International Settlements

March, 1971   *The Economics of Pollution*
Kenneth E. Boulding, Professor of Economics, University of Colorado
Elvis J. Stahr, President, National Audubon Society

Solomon Fabricant, Professor of Economics, New York University

Former Director, National Bureau of Economic Research

Martin R. Gainsbrugh, Adjunct Professor of Economics, New York University

Chief Economist, National Industrial Conference Board

April, 1971

Young America in the NOW World

Hubert H. Humphrey, Senator from Minnesota

Former Vice President of the United States

April, 1972

Optimum Social Welfare and Productivity: A Comparative View

Jan Tinbergen, Professor of Development Planning, Netherlands School of

Economics, Nobel Laureate

Abram Bergson, George E. Baker Professor of Economics, Harvard University

Fritz Machlup, Professor of Economics, New York University

April, 1973

Fiscal Responsibility: Tax Increases or Spending Cuts?

Paul McCracken, Edmund Ezra Day University Professor of Business Administration, University of Michigan

Murray L. Weidenbaum, Edward Mallinckrodt Distinguished University Professor, Washington University

Lawrence S. Ritter, Professor of Finance, New York University

Robert A. Kavesh, Professor

of Finance, New York University

March, 1974

Wall Street in Transition: The Emerging System and its Impact on the Economy

Henry G. Manne, Distinguished Professor of Law, Director of the Center for Studies in Law and Economics, University of Miami Law School

Ezra Solomon, Dean Witter Professor of Finance, Stanford University

March, 1975

Leaders and Followers in an Age of Ambiguity

George P. Schultz, Professor, Graduate School of Business, Stanford University; President, Bechtel Corporation

21

March, 1976   *The Economic System in an Age of Discontinuity: Long-Range Planning or Market Reliance?*
Wassily Leontief, Nobel Laureate, Professor of Economics, New York University
Herbert Stein, A. Willis Robertson Professor of Economics, University of Virginia

March, 1977   *Demographic Dynamics in America*
Wilber J. Cohen, Dean of the School of Education and Professor of Education and of Public Welfare Administration, University of Michigan
Charles F. Westhoff, Director of the Office of Population Research and Maurice During Professor of

Demographic   Studies,
Princeton University

March, 1978   *The Rediscovery of the Business Cycle*
Paul A. Volcker, President and Chief Executive Officer, Federal Reserve Bank of New York

March, 1979   *Economic Pressure and the Future of the Arts*
William Schuman, Composer
Rogert L. Stevens, Chairman of the Board of Trustees, John F. Kennedy Center for the Performing Arts

April, 1980   *Presidential Promises and Performance*
McGeorge Bundy, Professor of History, Faculty of Arts and Science, New York University
Edmund S. Muskie, Former

U.S. Senator from Maine,
Secretary of State

March, 1981

Econometric Models as Guides for Decision-Making
Lawrence R. Klein, Benjamin Franklin Professor of Finance and Economics, University of Pennsylvania, Nobel Laureate

March, 1982

The American Economy, 1960–2000
Richard M. Cyert, President, Carnegie-Mellon University

December, 1983

Reaganomics: Meaning, Means, and Ends
John Kenneth Galbraith, Paul M. Warburg Professor of Economics Emeritus, Harvard University
Paul W. McCracken, Ed-

mund Ezra Day Distinguished University Professor of BusinessAdministration, The University of Michigan, and Chairman, Council of Economic Advisers, American Institute for Public Policy Research

Note: All but the last seven volumes of The Charles C. Moskowitz Memorial Lectures were published by New York University Press. The 1977, 1978, 1979, 1980, 1981, 1982, and 1983 lectures were published by The Free Press.

The Joseph I. Lubin Memorial Lectures

March, 1984   *The World Banking System: Outlook in a Context of Crisis*
Andrew F. Brimmer, President of Brimmer & Com-

pany, Inc. and Chairman of the Monetary Policy Forum

December, 1984

The Deficits: How Big? How Long? How Dangerous?
Daniel Bell, Henry Ford II Professor of Social Sciences, Harvard University
Lester Thurow, Gordon Y. Billard Professor of Economics and Management, Massachusetts Institute of Technology

December, 1985

The Dollar, Debt, and the Trade Deficit
Anthony M. Solomon, Former Undersecretary of the Treasury, Former President and Chief Executive Officer of the Federal Reserve Bank of New York

March, 1987

The Strategic Defense Initiative: Its Effect on the

Economy and Arms Control
David Z. Robinson, Executive Vice President and Treasurer, Carnegie Corporation of New York

March, 1988

A Perspective on the Changing Business and Financial Environment
John J. Phelan, Jr., Chairman and Chief Executive Officer, New York Stock Exchange, Inc.

ACKNOWLEDGMENTS

I would like to thank Roger Kubarych, the Exchange's chief economist, for his important contribution to the preparation of this lecture, and to recognize the special help given by his associates Ira Gelb and Eileen Feibus, and visiting research fellow Wang Po Ming.

CONTENTS

CONTENTS

36

A PERSPECTIVE ON THE CHANGING BUSINESS AND FINANCIAL ENVIRONMENT

Introduction

It is a special privilege to speak before this distinguished group of scholars, students, and members of the business and financial community.

The Lubin Lectures have uniquely enriched our intellectual development. They have sharpened our collective understanding of important economic and financial issues and have made us think in new ways about the significance of those problems for public policy. It is a rare talent to be able to make sensible connections between concepts and practical courses of action, but the past Lubin lecturers have done that skillfully and cogently.

After October 1987's worldwide market decline, it seems as if everybody talks about markets. So much so that people begin to think that markets have an independent existence. Too often they seem to forget that the securities markets are a link in the chain that comprises the economic process.

My intention today is to assess the basic building blocks of our nation's longer-term competitive position: physical capital, human capital, and the financial markets which provide sustenance for both.

My guiding premise is that change is inevitable —in business and in the financial arena, as well as in government and in society at large. The global competitive environment mandates change, and over the next decade or so it will be more rapid than anything we have seen before. The rest of the world is working harder and getting smarter.

Consequently, if we are going to maintain the highest standard of living in the world for the largest number of people, we are going to have to do a number of tasks better than we have in the past. If we are going to be able to anticipate and manage change more effectively, we will have to build a more flexible, more responsive, and ultimately more productive economy. And that will not happen unless businesses and individuals themselves are more flexible, more adaptable, and more receptive to change.

If there is any one thing that we should teach the generations coming up, it is to be prepared to turn their lives upside down. To look at life not as a constant, but as a constantly moving, changing panorama in which they must find ways to help control that change for the betterment of society and the enrichment of their own lives.

To begin with, meeting the challenge of change entails substantial capital formation. That will involve large investments in business plants and equipment as well as new technology. It will involve equally large investments in all aspects of public infrastructure, especially our educational system.

It also means that we, as a nation, have to ask some uncomfortable questions about how to motivate people not only to work harder, but to work smarter and more cooperatively. We have to go back to the fundamentals about what strengths of resources, of organizational ability, and of work ethic have made the United States an economic powerhouse, and whether the formula is right for meeting the more exacting global competitive tests of the future.

Closer to where I live, it also entails asking some fundamental questions about whether the economy and the financial system are in harmony—whether the structure of the financial markets can adequately support the capital formation process, or whether the two have become uncoupled, as some believe.

I think it's fair to say that in some circles this questioning went on long before the stock market convulsions of October 1987. But, naturally, that trauma has provoked wider apprehension. Admittedly, much of this concern is focused solely on short-term consequences. So, if we can scrape by without slipping into recession and without suffering any large-scale financial failures, many will lose interest in questions about the structure of the financial markets. Nevertheless, a number of legitimate concerns about the long-term evolution of the financial markets and of market practices will deserve careful assessment.

I am troubled by a nagging feeling that an important sense of balance within the financial markets is endangered: the balance between the markets' fundamental role in supporting investment in the real economy and the role they play as a vehicle for largely speculative activity.

Good markets need both attributes. We need a properly functioning financial system in order to mobilize capital resources to support economic growth. We need dealers and other professional traders in order to provide the minute-to-minute and day-to-day liquidity that allows the public to feel comfortable participating in the market. Actively engaged professionals necessarily are risk takers, and that involves an element of speculation.

However, when the balance between investment support and speculation is upset, or even when it may only appear to have been upset, there is a potential for serious problems to arise.

Well-functioning equity markets play a uniquely important role in our financial system. They are the mechanism that helps to assure that scarce resources go into their most productive uses. They do that by providing an impersonal, and generally unbiased, yardstick for continuously evaluating the most productive uses of capital. Claims on capital, in turn, determine how investment funds are distributed among, and reallocated to, the industries that can use them most effectively.

Thus, equity markets encourage a happy marriage of capital raising and capital allocating, and, ultimately, help determine how national resources are used.

To get that remarkably powerful result, it is essential that the determination of relative values reflects a wide diversity of independent judgments on the part of millions of investors. A financial structure that is not based on diversity is going to play an imperfect (and, perhaps, occasionally counterproductive) role in allocating capital.

And if speculative elements were to predominate in markets like ours, which are generally free and open, then there is a very real danger that price formation can be overly influenced by the personal (and sometimes emotional) verdicts of a relative handful of professional money managers who control vast pools of funds. In that situation, even if resource allocation is not distorted, a sense of fairness that is essential for maintaining broad public confidence can be lost. Lose that, and the entire fabric which binds the financial system together is weakened.

To sum up these introductory remarks, tough questions need to be asked about how this nation is going to manage the difficult process of change in our economy and in our financial markets as the global climate becomes increasingly more competitive.

We are by no means starting from a position of extreme weakness; no objective review of the data would yield that exaggerated conclusion. But we are going to be hard-pressed to improve our performance in a number of critical areas in order to excell and, therefore, to prosper in a fast-changing, highly competitive environment.

Competitiveness: Concepts and History

Against this background, I would like to turn, first, to the concept of *competitiveness*.

An enormous amount has been written on the topic, a lot of agonizing has gone on over it, and yet misperceptions abound over what competitiveness is all about. Some of those misperceptions have had an unfortunate impact in coloring the policy views of a sizable portion of the public and their government representatives. Taken to an extreme, misguided policies toward international trade and investment could sadly push us in a direction that ultimately could jeopardize the continuation of open world markets. Thus, it is important to set out what the competitiveness problem is and what it isn't.

I think the most useful distinction to make is between what we might call "macro-competitiveness" or the relative competitiveness of the economy at large, with "micro-competitiveness" or the relative position of individual firms and industries.

Macro-competitiveness primarily has to do with broad economic aggregates and national savings behavior. The key determinant over the short run is the exchange rate. Essentially, movements in the exchange rate recalibrate the costs of goods and services here and abroad. In the world of the 1970s and 1980s, the enormous swings in exchange rates have far overwhelmed anything that could realistically be done to affect the competitive positions of individual firms *operating in the United States*.

Simply put, United States–located industry lost considerable ground during long stretches of that time period not because of bad management, poor technology, or weak products, but mainly because of an unrealistically high value of the dollar.

However, once you go beyond these almost cyclical swings in competitiveness caused by exchange rate movements, different questions arise. For example, how well does an American company do operating in Japan against indigenous Japanese companies? Or how well do Japanese companies, say auto companies, operating in the United States do against American car companies?

In these comparisons, the exchange rate effect washes out and what you are left with are, first, differences in capital investment and, second, the basic questions of management, organization, and incentives: In short, people—how they are trained, motivated, rewarded, and encouraged to work together.

This is what I call micro-competitiveness, and it is in this area where I believe the bulk of our most significant problems now lie.

With these distinctions in mind, it's worthwhile to look back over the recent historical experience of relative national competitiveness.

Coming out of World War II, the production capacity of this country was beyond the dream of anyone who had ever lived. We went to war in December 1941. By 1944, we had launched an incredible mass of equipment, planes, ships, and people, all those things that helped to win the war. Our industrial prowess was envied by everyone, particularly our enemies. Indeed, the Japanese were so impressed that, after the war, they asked if they could come here and study what we were doing and how we did it.

For most of the first two decades of the postwar period, it was rarely recognized, except by those with unusual vision, that U.S. manufacturing industry was destined to face severe competition and would have to adapt to a different global environment. Certainly, reconstruction was viewed as highly desirable and essentially inevitable. Major industrial countries abroad had come out of the war with vast destruction. Through sheer hard work and willpower they rebuilt their economies. They rebuilt them with modern, and often the best, technology and with workers who were skilled and dedicated.

Under these conditions, it wasn't thought to be a grave national problem that the U.S. share of, say, world steel production fell during the fifties and sixties, or that the U.S. share of world auto production declined during that period.

Quite the contrary. It was a tangible indication of the success of the strategy to reequip and re-energize those nations which would become known as the Western industrial democracies, including Japan. Nothing assured continued world peace and the growth of world trade more than that reconstruction.

In the meantime, praise was lavished on the management techniques and skills associated with U.S. multinational companies and, in no small measure, on U.S. business schools. Foreign journalists and scholars criticized their business executives for not meeting the American challenge by imitating our management techniques fast enough. They even founded business schools of their own!

By the late 1960s, however, concerns about U.S. competitiveness started to surface, once the European countries (and Japan, to a lesser extent) were seen to have more than caught up in a number of product areas. It slowly dawned on us that the underlying economics of the situation had changed.

Not everybody agreed, but most experts had come to the conclusion that the dollar had become overvalued relative to other major currencies. The yardstick was the basic production potential of the United States compared to that of the other industrial nations. We were slipping and differential cost and productivity trends were at the heart of it. Engineering a major shift in those costs through a depreciation of the dollar became the official U.S. policy thrust.

Trying to get exchange rates more or less in reasonable alignment turned out to be a tremendously contentious, and sometimes clumsy, process that took several years. And it never really was accomplished because in the middle of that process of recalibrating the world's competitive conditions from the perspective of exchange rates, all the industrial countries were hit—first, by successive oil price shocks and then by vast changes of economic values produced by the accelerating inflation of the 1970s.

Although the evidence is a little ambiguous in some respects, the U.S. competitive position did weaken to a significant extent during those years. Because of the veil of inflation, it looked like companies were making money, but those profits were largely illusory. However, the stock market stagnation of that time seemed to reflect economic reality.

It is worth remembering that the United States was not always the focal point of attention or concern. Even as recently as 1974, the world's financial leaders actually were most concerned about the competitive damage inflicted on Japan, a country which was seen to be inordinately vulnerable to flucuations in world trade and completely dependent on imported oil.

Of course, now we know what happened. The Japanese adjusted. In the process of adjusting, they brought to bear all their national strengths, specifically their cultural strengths, which coalesced into a force that created a surge in the competitiveness of Japanese products. In the process, a legacy of new problems was left behind which we have been struggling to contend with for the better part of a decade.

Libraries have been written about the Japanese success story, but it boils down to the two basic ingredients of economic growth that all nations need to develop: human capital and physical capital.

First, *people*. After 1950, the Japanese economy initially benefited from a monumental shift of the population out of agriculture and into the cities and, consequently, into manufacturing industry. This naturally yields big productivity improvements, but this type of gain doesn't accrue indefinitely.

Without a doubt, the most striking aspect of Japan's postwar modernization was the single-minded effort to raise the general educational level of the entire population.

The Japanese educational system had previously been essentially elitist, but modernization meant rapid enhancement of overall primary and secondary education. It retained respected values, however. The emphasis was on performance, high standards, and a belief in discipline and hard work. That broadened educational system soon produced a cadre of skilled workers who went into Japanese industry and didn't stop learning.

To its great credit, Japanese industry recognized early in the postwar period the importance of nurturing its human resources. Their early concern with employee development is exemplified by a Japanese study of a Ford Motor Company plant in Ohio in the late 1940s. The researchers spent three years at the plant and their conclusions, published in Japan in 1951, were rather extraordinary. They didn't talk about technology, or machines, or efficiency, what they talked about was the people they saw in that plant. They didn't have Ph.D.'s, but each worker knew his job, could modify the product that was coming through, and was free to make decisions on other matters as well.

Japanese business had established an incredibly extensive system of on-the-job training and development, highly structured and with uncompromising company support. Nearly half of all Japanese companies offer educational programs. To take one example, Sony practically runs a university of its own, offering wide-ranging training programs in foreign languages, finance, science, and engineering.

What is more, Japanese companies went one step further to train people in the intangibles: character building, knowledge of company history and values, and the ability to work with others.

What was the tangible result of this national and corporate philosophy of educational advancement? A remarkable ability to adjust quickly to new economic realities. That adjustment capability was particularly apparent in the Japanese response to the two oil shocks. The evidence was a productivity record which, while understandably less sparkling than in the cheap-energy, high-growth 1960s, was still impressive by international standards—at 5.5 percent per annum, it was three times better than what the United States was achieving.

Throughout this period, Japan was able to mobilize huge amounts of domestic *savings* to support the second crucial ingredient for powerful economic growth, *physical capital formation.* The share of output going for business-fixed investment throughout the post–oil-shock period remained extraordinarily high, averaging nearly 20 percent of GNP for private plant and equipment expenditures —just about double what we were doing in this country.

Capital formation—by raising capacity, cutting costs, introducing new technology, and lowering oil vulnerability through energy conservation—equipped Japan with a manufacturing base that was virtually unrivaled, hardly a decade after Japan's competitive position was viewed as precarious. And, what is more significant, it was a manufacturing sector that was not only generating impressive growth rates, but was universally regarded as producing some of the best quality products anywhere in the world.

Sources of Productivity Improvement

I believe it is useful to assess productivity improvement by making a simple conceptual distinction. Productivity can best be thought of in two parts. First is what economists call ''embodied technical progress.'' In other words, install a new machine that contains within it more advanced technology than an old machine, and, as a result, the productivity of the process will increase. With Japanese capital formation at rates sometimes more than double those of the United States in many industries, it was inevitable that embodied technical progress was going to lift their productivity at a more rapid rate.

Much of that technical progress was imported. Japan did not have a myopic nationalistic view of technology (in sharp contrast to its attitudes toward finished products). It had an internationalist view. Japanese companies scoured the world to get what was worthwhile and what worked. More often than we like to admit, much of that technology came out of the United States and came relatively cheaply— through licensing arrangements and other contractural relationships. And we shouldn't underestimate the contribution made by the large number of young Japanese who came home, having been through major American universities and engineering institutes, and helped speed the transfusion of that new technology.

All this underscores an important fact: While Japan's rate of capital formation was about double that of the United States, its rate of productivity growth was about three times as fast. Accounting for that part of productivity improvement which is *not* embodied in new capital has long puzzled economists all over the world. How does it happen? I might add that this question has been known to puzzle stock analysts trying to figure out which companies are going to outperform others.

"Disembodied technical progress" seems to be an apt term for the phenomenon. But we all know it as productivity gains that come from better organization, better design, or management initiatives —or just from working smarter.

Whatever the terminology, it's a function of people: The way they are trained, the way they are organized, and the way they view and go about their jobs.

In the case of the Japanese, you saw a visible manifestation of how a well-educated and then continuously trained labor force can cooperate to make a string of incremental improvements in the way things are done in the workplace.

The result was not only economic growth of a quantitative nature, merely adding up what got produced, but economic growth in a qualitative sense, creating products that were widely considered advanced, reliable, and good value for the money.

Experts debate how much of this outcome reflects intrinsically Japanese traits and how much can be generalized. My suspicion is that there may be some aspects of the Japanese experience that simply cannot be adopted by others because of cultural differences. But much more of what they are doing successfully can be emulated.

As a matter of fact, if you go to many of the high-wage, high-productivity countries in Europe, you often see much the same pattern. There is a highly educated work force, though it may not be organized so formally around the group or the team as in Japan. But you will see many of the same kind of intelligent, productivity-enhancing, incremental changes at the work-floor level that you find in Japan.

Whatever the cultural background, the key to nurturing better productivity is to do more than just installing sophisticated capital equipment and treating it primarily as a way of reducing the number of employees. The critical factor is the ability to mobilize the commitment and talent of people at all levels, not just the top technicians and managers.

I think I can put it all together by telling you a story. Some time ago, my wife, Joyce, and I were in Japan and were invited to visit a Toyota plant in

Nagoya, an industrial city on the plain of Honshu. At the plant they start the manufacturing process with raw material and three days later, have a completed car on a ship to Yokohama headed for a competitive market overseas. That plant was as modern as possible.

But beyond that, the workers were committed to the task and to their company. They worked on the assembly line six days a week and the seventh day played baseball for the company team or their division team or both. That "esprit de corps" is only the beginning!

The plant had just been redesigned to raise the production platform so the cars that came down the production line could be worked on more easily. The reason it was done was that all the assembly line workers sat down in groups and asked: How can we be more competitive? How can we produce a better car? How can we make it faster? Their response was that the platform must be raised; and it was, at a cost of several million dollars.

There were eighteen work stations on the platform. As a car came down the assembly line, the workers at each work station checked the work that was done at the previous station and then did their own work. When a flaw was found, they pushed a button which activated an alarm bell and the entire plant stopped.

If that flaw was not fixed within one minute, a team of five engineers would descend on that station in a matter of minutes and nothing in that plant would move until the defect was fixed. Once it was fixed, a signal was given and the assembly line moved again.

When it came to putting the steering wheel in, it was marked left or right. It made no difference in the assembly operation. All that had to be done was to stick the steering column on the appropriate side of the chassis. In Japan they ride on the left side of the road like the British; still they made sure that cars produced for export to the U.S. were adapted for the American market. In contrast, I don't know of any American cars imported into Japan that are equipped with right-side steering.

I think that the most important part of the Nagoya plant's experience is something the Japanese learned at that Ford plant I mentioned earlier; the important element is not technology. Rather it is the skill, intelligence, and interest of the workers who felt a partnership and a pride in the production process that really delivered the car that conquered the automobile world.

Is this approach found in the United States? Absolutely. And probably far more extensively than many critics would have us believe. Many Japanese executives I have met assert that U.S. business invented the notion of worker involvement in "quality circles" and the encouragement of personal efforts to improve the productivity of the group. We invented it, but the Japanese embraced it.

The loss of market share both at home and abroad finally set companies like Ford to talking about quality, quality, quality. Ford looked back to 1951 to rediscover what the Japanese had learned from them and to reapply it in the 1980s. They began to talk with organized labor as partners and not as adversaries.

While worker involvement is a growing trend, we clearly still have a lot of work to do.

We began to take down the old industrial infrastructure and build anew. Large integrated plants exemplified by the River Rouge Plant of the Ford Motor Company, at one time the pride and symbol of our industrial might, have been disassembled and parts production has been dispersed among smaller, more efficient units.

Parts producers are no longer big companies but small companies, and those small companies are beginning to do things that the Japanese have done and what we had taught the Japanese years ago. U.S. producers are beginning to use a different kind of work ethic. They actively involve people in different ways, including making workers partners in company decision making as the Japanese have done. But more importantly, they are making workers financial partners as well.

The recession of 1982, painful as it was, made companies in this country far leaner and impressed them with the need to keep pressure on costs. They stepped up investment in new plant and equipment, as well as in the modernization of existing plant and equipment.

All of that provides evidence that old attitudes have been changing in this country and new attitudes have been coming in: new competitive attitudes, new ways of doing things, new kinds of plants, and the retooling of old plants. Indeed, the New York Stock Exchange is also involved in this trend. We, too, have taken an old plant and retooled it.

In the same physical plant that in 1968 did 16 million shares a day, we had two days in October 1987 in which we did 600 million shares each. We would like to handle that volume level better and we will handle it better, but the point is that the increase in the productivity of our plant has been absolutely incredible. The lesson we've learned is that while physical capital is very, very important, more and more the watchword of the late eighties and nineties is going to be "people capital"—a greater emphasis on people.

You can learn about people capital if you go to the Silicon Valley area around Palo Alto, California. There are literally hundreds of companies that are not consciously copying the Japanese, have re-learned what we knew in this country many years ago—that is, making everybody a partner.

One such company is called Tandem Computers, started up in 1975. When I first learned of Tandem in 1977, it had modest sales, but it had a computer that was well suited for trading systems. After a lot of talk about whether we could count on the viability of such a small company, we decided to go ahead and put our equipment investment in Tandem products. It was the right decision. One of the reasons that we are able to do the volume we are doing today is partly due to Tandem.

Tandem is a very, very unusual company. In 1977, when we first did business with it and were its first major customer, it had $60 million in sales.

It has over a billion dollars in sales today, has seven or eight plants in this country, and plants in Europe and the Far East.

When I first visited Tandem, I couldn't tell who the manager was because everybody was wearing a T-shirt and dungarees. One of the interesting things about their operation is that the production people and the engineers intermix all the time. A production person putting together a computer would call over an engineer and say: "Look at this; I've got to make this piece and I've got to reach around the computer to work on it. You've got it on the wrong side; move it over to the other side so I can do my job better."

They have developed a corporate culture in which every Friday, at every Tandem facility all the workers take a break at three o'clock in the afternoon. In short, they stop what they are doing and get to know their fellow workers.

For them, the break is an engaging way of lowering communications barriers. It mixes everybody in the company and allows them to share ideas. And Tandem is but one of hundreds and hundreds of companies that have sprung up in this country in the last ten years or so, that have spearheaded the move to worker involvement.

Though we've started down the right road, we clearly have a lot of work to do before we can be satisfied with the extent of our commitment to involving all levels of a company in the goal of making the business more productive.

The U.S. Economic Record

Having said that, it would be wrong to disregard the positive record of U.S. business over the past several years. Since the trough of the last recession in 1982, the economy has grown at very satisfactory rates. The expansion is one of the longest in our history. Most sectors contributing to economic growth have done notably better than in the 1970s. That was not so difficult to accomplish immediately coming out of a recession, but it has been more difficult to accomplish during the more mature phases of the expansion.

It suggests that there should be considerable confidence that the various components of our economic system have the ability to respond to valid economic incentives. And we are no longer handicapped by some of the previous impediments to growth—high inflation and excessively costly and unstable energy sources. *So there are strong positive signs in the current situation.*

First, job creation is clearly impressive, especially when compared to other major countries. We have added 15 million jobs since 1980; by comparison, Europe as a whole has lost 1 million, while Japan has added only about 4 million. This has been a powerful force helping to sustain economic expansion. Today, over 62 percent of our working-age population is employed; this is several percentage points higher than the average for other industrial countries. It reflects favorable demographics and social changes that have made it more acceptable for women to go into the work force and seek challenging assignments. And it reflects reasonably liberal immigration policies, and that peculiarly American strength to absorb people from all over the world and bring them into our labor force with their skills, their ambition, their sense of optimism, and their dreams.

The job creation record is even more notable when you consider that it was done without the help of the *Fortune 500* companies who have, in fact, lost jobs on balance. We've done that through all those innovative companies that are springing up and all those companies that have been rejuvenating themselves over a period of time. As foreigners look at us and criticize this country's policies, they also say it is a wonder that we have put so many people to work. We have the kind of entrepreneurial spirit that is continuing to boost jobs after five and one-half years without a recession.

Second, business investment. We've started to install more physical capital. Admittedly, the early phase of that expansion was partly policy induced. Changes in the tax code in the early 1980s effectively subsidized some forms of business investment, through accelerated depreciation and an expanded investment tax credit. Those incentives worked. Businesses responded. Plant and equipment expenditures got stronger.

Now that those incentives have been repealed, there are other factors moving in the direction of stimulating capital formation. Clearly, the most influential factor is the significant decline in the value of the dollar since 1985. Those manufacturing companies that went through the trauma of an excessive, and unpredicted, rise in the value of the dollar had to shift their priorities from expansion to survival. But in the process, many of those companies were able to do a number of things to improve their productivity and lower their costs throughout that period. They had to.

But, it now appears that at least part of the damage is reversible. Now that the dollar is down, and down a lot, we are seeing clear evidence of a gradual firming of U.S. export orders, an improvement in export volume, and some improvement in competition against imports. These are trends that are leading to higher capacity utilization and a growing need for more capacity.

For the time being, capital spending is likely to remain under careful scrutiny because of uncertainties about the immediate economic outlook. While most manufacturing companies expect to go forward with their current investment plans, they are proceeding cautiously. There will probably be fewer brand new or what are called ''green fields'' investments, and more targeted investments to extend capacity in existing plants, remove bottlenecks in the production process, and hold down production costs. Incidentally, that is exactly the tack we are taking at the NYSE to raise our capacity.

I suspect that the longer-term direction of U.S. investment is fairly solid. When we see capacity utilization rates above 80 or 85 percent—and even higher for some industries—we know that older, less efficient plants are being put to use. Their technical limitations and cost implications soon are obvious to everyone.

Not all sectors are benefiting. A few industries, like home and office building, will feel contractionary pressures for some time. But we are now beginning to see a kind of renaissance in the manufacturing sector, especially in those industrial areas that not so long ago were branded the "rust bowl."

To be sure, not every manufacturing company is out of danger. However, the improvement in overall conditions bodes well for a virtuous cycle of stronger investment, faster implantation of new technology, better productivity, more profitability, and an increased capability of attracting financial capital into manufacturing.

To sum up this section. We've had healthy economic growth during the last several years. And the recent revival in our manufacturing sector ought to put to rest some of the alarmist and clearly exaggerated cries of deindustrialization by people who ought to have known better. We are getting a desirable shift of resources to the goods-producing industries, which is essential for eventually reducing our trade deficit. The evidence seems to be emerging that what I've referred to as the "macro-competitiveness" of the U.S. economy is improving.

While we can be generally positive about the prospects for better economic performance over, say, the next ten or fifteen years, there are still a number of difficult decisions that have to be made before we can be confident about putting behind us many of the concerns that have overhung the financial market in recent years. Among them are concerns about our ability to reduce our federal budget deficit, about our ability to eliminate the trade deficit (however encouraging recent numbers appear), and about our ability to generate domestic savings to support adequate capital formation.

Essentially, these are all problems of underlying imbalances in economic and financial conditions. Balance also has to be restored in a number of other important relationships before we can be assured of achieving continuing improvement in productivity at what I have called the "micro-competitive" level.

I would put particular stress on seeking improvements in two important areas: First, in the balance between investment in physical capital and investment in human capital; and second, in the ability of those of us involved in the financial markets to structure them in a way that adequately supports the overall capital formation process—and that means significantly improving the balance of forces in the marketplace in order to reduce financial instability.

Questions About U.S. Education

Turning to the question of human capital, the evidence is mounting that our educational system is failing to produce a competitive work force for the future. It is failing not because of a letup in the quality of research at our top universities and research institutes, nor in the level of creativity, or the caliber of their graduates. They are a magnet for students the world over to learn in all areas of science, technology, management skills, and so on.

That educational complex, the university scientific-technological apparatus, is well funded, and American business has played an important role in maintaining that funding. Foreign commentators who look at our educational system start out by praising that scientific-technological educational complex before they go on to make their real criticisms.

Where they detect a growing problem, and I concur, is in the area of general education—the educational standards and expectations which reach that large majority of the population that is not going to end up in our major universities, research institutes, and business schools.

Putting aside the personal and social implications, you simply cannot run a country properly and have a good productive work force without a sound educational base. It does not mean that you need armies of Ph.D.'s. The Japanese didn't develop enormous university systems; they developed enormous secondary and high school systems so that everybody in Japan had to go to high school, everybody had to become literate and have a good grounding in basic skills. They do have a culture that is probably more amenable to direction. So our job will be tougher.

But we do have an earlier American tradition of educational excellence. At one time, we had a very, very good public school system; the polar opposite of today's educational crisis. We have to rethink across-the-board what we are doing about general education in this country.

This rethinking is surely needed for our inner-city schools. But I believe responsible leaders in government and the business community now grasp the urgency of those problems. They are enormously complicated and no one who has given any thought to the dimensions of the task has any illusions about the amount of resources that will be required simply to bring standards up to barely tolerable levels.

But it is not solely a financial issue. What is at stake is a basic problem of society, specifically the matter of drugs. The problem is nationwide in scope. But, it takes on a special dimension in many inner-city neighborhoods. There, a powerful and pervasive drug economy is unfortunately firmly implanted. The incentive structure we normally associate with our enterprise economy has been co-opted and then warped by what goes on in that drug economy. It is not subterranean, either. Young people in the inner cities often see no competing incentive structure that seems to deliver the material results that the drug business flashes before them. The effect is debilitating, sapping any motivation for real learning that would equip the kids for jobs in the mainstream economy. Of course, we should demand that this drug business be stopped. But until that can happen, dealing with the educational deficiencies of the inner city will take on added complexity.

But the inner-city schools are not the only problem, and in many ways they may be susceptible to a more rapid turnaround. The more difficult problem to reverse may actually lie with the average schools, particularly those where parents and local taxpayers are self-satisfied and not aware of any blatant deficiencies.

Is the U.S. educational system improving on the average or are we just marking time? Look at ordinary schools in typical middle-class neighborhoods around the country. Are they demanding the science, the mathematics, and the foreign language training—even the training in the proper use of our own language—that the U.S. business of the year 2000 will require from employees at every level of the organization? Are we developing a culture in our schools that promotes collective, group efforts to solve problems, the skills that are needed in the workplace? Or are we still looking at education strictly in individualistic terms, with little regard to developing the modes of cooperative behavior that the business world will increasingly demand?

Furthermore, we have to be concerned about

73

whether our approach to education has become too inward-looking, too parochial. Are we sufficiently open to the good educational ideas that other countries are using successfully? Put another way, are educators here giving enough thought to the kinds of skills that people are bringing to the workplace in other countries and the kinds of educational techniques that are being used to build those skills?

This type of assessment will naturally raise some highly controversial topics. Take the simple matter of how long our schools are open. Can we really afford to close our schools for three months a year when the Japanese and many European schools are open for instruction for ten or eleven months? This vestige of our nineteenth-century agricultural economy may not be a luxury the twenty-first century will permit us if we want to stay at the top.

Admittedly, the answer is not to slavishly replicate another country's entire school system. No one is seriously arguing for radical change like that. But we have to recognize that we have a more educationally oriented economy and a more competitive environment worldwide. The United States has a school system that predates that situation and is based on a time when we enjoyed a commanding position in the world.

Some of the measures of our performance are highly disturbing. Less than 50 percent of our high school seniors can read at levels considered barely adequate for carrying out a battery of simple tasks. Measures of writing ability are far worse. At the level of basic literacy, the United States ranks an embarrassing fifty-ninth out of 158 United Nations members.

U.S. business pays a heavy price for this. As David Kearns, the chairman of Xerox Corporation, put it recently, "The U.S. educational system has been producing a whole generation of handicapped workers. They are handicapped because they cannot read, they cannot write, they cannot do mathematics and they do not know foreign languages."

Executives of our local telephone company, NY-NEX, have stated that when they tried to fill a variety of job openings over a recent period, 23,000 candidates applied, but only about 15 percent of them could pass a relatively simple test of basic reading and arithmetic. Other examples abound, but I think the general picture is clear.

If the Japanese experience and our own experience are correct, we need a combination of effective public education and business training of employees. We are terribly deficient in both and we have got to put an incredible amount of resources into education in the next ten years or so.

To say we need more doesn't mean that I don't acknowledge the enormous efforts on the part of both public and private education and business to change things. One notable example of business and government cooperation is the Boston Compact.

Businesses in Boston, the mayor of Boston, and the educational system there literally signed a compact to guarantee jobs, both for high school graduates and for summer employment. As a quid pro quo, the school system agreed to cut absenteeism, cut the drop-out rate and increase academic standards. Moreover, they set annual improvement targets.

The Boston Compact was so successful that the English, who—despite their success in turning their economy around—still have problems in their old industrial cities, borrowed the plan. In London, 200 corporations are participating in an exact duplicate of the Boston Compact. If it works there, plans are to implement it in Manchester, Liverpool, Glasgow, and other industrial centers.

Plainly, business cannot afford to wait for the products of an overhauled school system. Self-interest alone dictates that business acts to improve its very uneven record in supporting the education and training of employees. Too few companies run any systematic educational programs, unlike companies in Japan and elsewhere.

The typical excuse is that job turnover is so high, it doesn't pay for an individual company to devote resources to this kind of effort. But a recent study of Japanese turnover rates (which average about one-fourth of ours) indicates that there is a direct positive relationship between the amount of training a company does and the probability of retaining a worker. Training seems to build a significant amount of company loyalty as it builds a lot of human capital.

If our schools and businesses are not doing the job of educating and training as well as they could, it is legitimate to ask how we expect to be able to maintain a well-prepared work force capable of confronting vigorous foreign competition ten or twenty years from now.

No doubt, the top technicians, the top engineers, and the top business managers will continue to design and install new machines that embody the best technology, even if it must be bought abroad. But the best technology alone won't ensure productivity growth. While the people at the top can furnish the technology, they alone can't make sure it's used most productively. They can't make the little changes in procedures that make a difference; they can't guarantee the attention to detail that drives quality. Those values have to be instilled in every employee and that takes dedicated training. A casual, perfunctory training program shortchanges the company, the worker, and our national economy.

The payoff is attested to by a number of studies that show a correlation between business investment in training and employee productivity. In principle, the stock market will notice that over time, and farsighted companies will enjoy improving stock values which will draw capital to them. That sets a virtuous circle in motion. Better, cheaper access to capital enables those companies to invest more. That investment allows installation of the best technology. Add to that a flexible, well-trained work force, and we are dealing with the potential for a very satisfactory outcome for the company and for the economy's long-term competitiveness.

But, however much business can contribute to the process of building human capital, we have to bear in mind the fact that what will come out of the educational system in the year 2000, in terms of the basic abilities young people will bring to the workplace, is already in the pipeline. For today's elementary students, there is still time. For today's high school students, there is little that can be done to significantly change the thrust of their education. That heightens the need for company training programs.

Every year we stay complacent or argue over minor details yields another group of students who will come to work poorly equipped to meet the challenges of the workplace. We are, therefore, wasting enormous potential by failing to act.

As the Japanese observed in their 1951 study of the Ford plant, educated workers who get to know the product, who could redesign the product, who could input into the design of production facilities, and take pride in their work are the key to success. That is where our competitors are today and where our future should lie. Our people are our hope for realizing the promise of the new industrial revolution. How successfully we come through this industrial revolution is not going to depend on natural resources, but on educational resources and the resourcefulness with which we apply them.

Restoring Better Balance in the Financial Markets

"Get me the right people and I will find you a business" is an old but very, very true saying. But you also need financing and you need financial markets to help raise it.

An appropriate conclusion to my presentation is an assessment of how capable the financial markets are of supporting the ambitious program of capital formation which we need in order to strengthen our competitive position in the world.

Before presenting my somewhat technical assessment, I want to capture for you the essence of what the financial markets are all about by relating a story about the development of a company which I'm sure most of you know—Mrs. Fields' Cookies.

Mrs. Fields, a housewife in her late twenties with two children, began to think that maybe she would like to do something more in life. She thought and asked all her friends about what she could do well. The thing she did best in this world, she concluded, was bake cookies—chocolate-chip cookies. So, she borrowed $50,000 from her husband, listened to a lot of ridicule from her friends, and opened a cookie store in Palo Alto, California, the heart of the high-tech capital.

First day, she had not one customer. Next morning, Mrs. Fields went up and down the main street of Palo Alto, which is not too big, and handed out cookies. She never wanted for a customer again. She opened branches, first in California, then all over the country. Then, she wanted to open stores all over the world. To finance these expansion plans, she decided to go public.

Mrs. Fields chose to go public in London rather than in this country. There, she could get a higher price-earnings ratio—that is, she could raise more money per dollar of profit—than she could in the U.S. market to improve and expand the company.

Mrs. Fields' story illustrates what financial markets are for. They allowed a young woman with a seemingly simplistic idea—baking chocolate-chip cookies for sale—to form a business, provide employment, make employees shareholders, and offer investors a new investment opportunity.

Unfortunately, soon after Mrs. Fields' stock was issued, its price plummeted, indicating it had been overpriced in London. But there are competitive markets in this country and London and an inter-play of market forces between the two. Soon the market valuations of Mrs. Fields' stock in London and the U.S. converged. As the company straight-ened itself out, new financing opportunities became available in both markets.

Mrs. Fields' cookie company has purchased other companies and now is a diversified food business that is continuing to grow.

October 22, 1987, I got a letter from Mrs. Fields saying she was delighted that we were able to weather the storm. She also said that she hoped to be listed on the New York Stock Exchange some-day and that anytime I wanted, she would provide 220 chocolate-chip cookies to any function that I would like. But free cookies are not why I've re-lated the Mrs. Fields story.

To me, her experience is a story about capital markets. Markets are to raise capital, to allocate capital, to serve new businesses, to help them grow, to help entrepreneurs, and to help established busi-nesses recondition, refurbish themselves, and grow further.

Financial markets are not primarily speculative markets, they are not tools for certain people to make money at the expense of everybody else. And they are not a way to grab a quick buck. They serve an important function in this country. In combination with physical capital and people capital, the function of our financial markets is to raise the American standard of living.

It is widely recognized that without well-functioning financial markets, capital formation will be stunted and capital resources will fail to be attracted to their most productive uses. Those inefficiencies would, over a long period of time, erode our economic potential and leave us seriously weakened as an international competitor.

Thus, it is essential that we critically evaluate the structure of our financial markets and the multiple roles that they play in raising capital, allocating resources, and encouraging the effective and responsible management of existing assets.

How these roles are carried out is now acutely conditioned by the rapid evolution of the world's financial system. The search for financial capital to support investment in structures, equipment, and research has become global. And large, sophisticated global capital markets have developed to meet those needs. Thus, pools of savings wherever they exist are increasingly becoming available on a worldwide basis.

It is fast becoming archaic to speak about a domestic market meeting domestic capital formation needs, except where poor creditworthiness has impaired access to the global pool of funds.

These global financial markets are not perfectly integrated at this point; perhaps they can never be. But the linkages are highly developed. The technologies employed are converging rapidly. And the thought processes of the market participants are looking more and more alike.

What it means is that stresses in one segment of the global financial network, for instance the foreign exchange markets, quickly set off impulses that drive reactions in other types of markets, whether the government bond market or the equities market. The potential for fast transmission of these impulses is vastly increased by technology and by virtually instantaneous access to essentially the same information—at least under all but the most unsettled market conditions.

As a result, the probability that any new scrap of information will touch off significant shifts in expectations is substantially increased. Trading patterns or strategies can change at any moment. And the entire step-jump in responsiveness can trigger off a degree of volatility in interest rates, exchange rates, or equity prices that few would have believed possible ten or twenty years ago.

The marketplace does not fabricate the impulses that lead to pronounced swings in sentiment and, therefore, prices and trading activity. As long as we have uncertainty about underlying economic growth, about the economic policies that the different countries pursue, about imbalances in trade, in national saving rates, and in governemnt budgets, then, understandably, financial markets are going to remain vulnerable to sudden shifts in market judgments. That means volatility is likely to stay high indefinitely. We've got to accept that as a basic constraint with which we must work.

One of the direct consequences of this kind of world is that forces that might otherwise contribute to balance or equilibrium in the markets tend to be weakened, and there is a danger of lasting erosion in the overall depth and resiliency of the financial markets.

The way it works is this: The higher the velocity of transactions and the more volatile the movement in asset values, the more dealers or position takers are attracted to the system. That is simply a reflection that the market needs the counteractive (or call it speculative) element in order to provide liquidity to those more intermittent users of the market who have to have the ability to shed risk.

But if the velocity of transactions and the price volatility associated with it surpass what is viewed as normal bounds, there is a danger that the speculative element will begin to overwhelm the system as a whole. At that point, there is a threat that smaller, less-frequent users of the market will withdraw on the assumption that dealers and other professionals have superior information and that there is no longer a level playing field where all can compete on equal terms. Take that to the logical extreme, and the relative share of a small number of large players will start to rise to worrisome proportions.

The burden on the regulators is to try to retain as much of the balance between professionals and smaller, less-frequent market participants as possible without subjecting the dealer or the speculative element to such stringent inhibitions that the benefits of their participation are lost.

Thus, the guiding principle must be to ensure that as much information as possible is available on a timely basis to all prospective participants in the marketplace so that no small group of large participants can achieve a persistent advantage. The goal must be to diffuse the technology to permit equal access to information, not to try somehow to suppress the technology or legislate it away.

As I listen to the conclusions of those experts who reviewed the dramatic events in the market in October 1987 and read their reports, I am struck by the common theme of frustration with the unavailability of reliable information during the worst moments of the crisis. The way I would put it, the market can stand anything but not knowing.

When information is imperfect, the natural remedy would seem to be mechanisms to close the knowledge gap, whether about the magnitude of order imbalances in individual stocks or about the levels of prices at which participants would be willing to trade. That is the logic behind the use of trading halts and delayed openings at the New York Stock Exchange. They are mechanisms designed to allow information to become available to the largest possible number of potential market participants.

I suppose that they might also be viewed as prototypes of so-called "circuit breakers," an approach the Brady Commission Report endorsed. I've been thinking about the metaphor "circuit breakers" and wonder whether a somewhat different analogy might be useful to consider as we ponder ways to improve the stability of the system.

Circuit breakers prevent overloaded electric circuits from causing fires. But when a surge of power causes a circuit breaker to flip off, the lights along the line go out. And they don't go back on until the source of the power surge is identified and fixed.

In the kind of interdependent, interconnected international financial system we now have, it might be better to think not so much in terms of a single electrical line in our house, but in terms of something more akin to the power grid that connects all the electrical systems of a large region into a unified network. When a piece of the grid has a problem, you don't turn off all the power. You isolate that part of the grid where the problem seems to lie and modulate the electric flow into that sector. The lights will dim, but they won't all go out.

As we design shock absorbers for periods of extraordinary volatility, we want to preserve the power grid analogy as much as we can. If we lean toward cutting the line, then we will simply encourage market participants to do the business they want to do in another way, or in another sector of the worldwide grid—say, in London or in Tokyo.

I suppose one example of this modulation approach is the rule recently adopted by the New York Stock Exchange that allows us to restrict the access of program trades to our order routing systems when there is a 50-point movement up or down in the Dow Jones average during a given day. Bursts of program trading, especially those associated with arbitrage between the stock index futures markets and the stock market, have occasionally been a source of unsettlement for the equities markets generally. The resulting volatility tends to deter participation by a large number of small investors, individuals and institutions alike, and, thus, can ultimately detract from the equities market's fundamental role of valuing companies and setting up the incentives for capital to move toward its best uses. We all suffer when the equities market can't fulfill that function.

However useful such a rule may be, it is not designed to be a panacea for volatility. The underlying source of volatility comes from unstable expectations. Large investors seek to sell large numbers of their futures contracts in a short period of time because they see something happening in the overall economy or economic policy climate that unsettles them. So the fundamental situation has to be to get the economics right.

It is reasonable to consider what more could be done to alleviate some manifestations of unsettlement in our markets. The reality is that we have a highly institutionalized market and the institutions' share is growing. The individual investor is still involved in the financial markets, but has made choices which lead to enhanced institutionalization. Thus, the use of mutual funds has grown, and the reliance on various forms of contractual savings, which tend to pool funds, has increased.

As a result, buying and selling decisions are being concentrated in the hands of a limited number of people who are responsible for tremendous sums of money. They are fiduciaries, and they must manage those funds prudently and in the full interest of their clients.

Fair enough. But they also have a public responsibility. They have a responsibility to the market. They and others need the market to be there and operating fairly and efficiently tomorrow, next week, next year, and years from now as well. So in their buying and selling decisions involving large sums of money, they ought to be taking the public interest into account. That means they must think not only about today's trade, but about the mechanism by which trading can be perpetuated.

Can they do that without an elaborate, and what would probably be a highly cumbersome and counterproductive network of controls and regulations? That is to be seen. We will watch and see whether a new element can be brought into the investment decision process that will tend to lead to a heightened sense of responsibility manifested in more judicious responses to changes in expectation or opinion. That would be constructive because it would tend to spread out the buying or selling impulses over a period of time.

I'm not entirely optimistic that this is possible unless values change, unless corporate cultures change. The investment attitudes that matter most, of course, are those held by the corporate executives who hire the money managers. Too often they impose on them exacting performance requirements that generate exactly the kind of in-and-out trading behavior which can be most destructive of the value of the shares in the very companies that are doing the hiring of those money managers. This shortsighted orientation toward performance needs reassessment. In the meantime, a certain sense of understanding is needed that what one large investor does can have a direct impact on the status of the overall market. Hopefully, October 1987's experience is enough of a lesson to imbue large institutions with that fundamental understanding.

If financial markets are operating properly and we have in the equities markets a more reasoned approach to decision making, then we have major ingredients in place to provide a climate in which capital formation for the future can be encouraged. But that's not enough. There also has to be a change in attitudes toward equity financing.

This is a very controversial area, and thoughtful people differ. No one can say with certainty what the capital structure of corporations ought to look like. And practices vary enormously across countries.

But, looking ahead, if one of our guiding principles is to manage change more effectively and create a more flexible economic structure, it seems prudent to have more equity in the system and less debt.

People, including prominent senators and congressmen, often ask what can be done to encourage equity financing and to increase the ratios of equity to debt. It's an important question and I wish there were an easy answer to it. There are great pitfalls to any of the potential routes by which greater incentives could be given to equity financing.

One of those highly controversial routes is to change the tax code in order to treat at least some portion of companies' dividend payments on the same tax deductible basis as their interest payments on debt. Part of the reason debt financing has become so prominent is simply because of tax considerations. But I don't sense a major initiative in this direction any time soon. There is considerable resistance, even among corporate executives, to a system that would tend to make them compete more overtly on the basis of dividend payments.

But clearly, the biggest obstacle to equity financing right now is straightforward. The stock market is down from its August 1987 high. Even at the historic levels reached in August 1987, there was no outpouring of plans to float new equity issues, perhaps because companies just didn't want to give the investing public the impression that they thought that the market had topped. This leads to a general conclusion that unless you have a more systematic process of issuing equities, you'll always be stymied to a certain extent by the concern that you will give an unintended, unwelcome, signal to current and potential shareholders alike that the stock price has gone up too much.

Consequently, while the future role of equity in

the financing of existing companies will probably increase moderately, there are huge obstacles to achieving a far greater role for equity even under the best of circumstances. Of course, current market conditions make the situation worse not only for existing companies, but for all kinds of smaller, up-and-coming companies that would like to go public. Confidence has been severely undermined. It's going to take a long process of careful and patient rebuilding to restore the kind of confidence we thought we had not too long ago. That means attention to many of the structural elements in the marketplace—some of which have been addressed with great seriousness by the various studies of the market decline.

Based on my own review of these studies, without getting into specific details, I conclude there is a strong case for rationalizing financial regulation where the underlying product is the same and simply appears in various forms in different marketplaces. Equity products deserve one overseer, a primary regulator that can harmonize the different technical aspects of detailed regulation, which necessarily will vary from marketplace to marketplace, and set them against a broader public policy concern. The public will restore its confidence in the stock market when they feel that the authorities charged with maintaining sound, flexible, and fair markets are acting coherently in the public interest.

The SEC, the traditional and experienced overseer of stocks and stock markets, logically comes to mind for the role of harmonizer, and it may come to that at some point in the future. In the meantime, there shouldn't be any opposition by thoughtful people to better coordination among the different regulators who do have the prescribed roles of today. It could be that the impetus for better coordination requires some prodding, perhaps from Congress; or maybe it can occur spontaneously, because it makes sense.

Either way, better coordination would enhance the planning process. It would better equip us all to deal with contingencies which may seem remote, but which, if considered ahead of time, could be handled effectively and smoothly should they happen. At times, coordination could be used more purposefully to modify technical regulations so that we actually arrive at a level playing field. That is important and would be useful.

Many have been asking lately whether, after all is said and done, we have already arrived at "one market," where all activities are conjoined in a unified whole; or whether there continue to be distinct and separable marketplaces—each with its own independent sources of liquidity serving identifiably different needs and purposes for different classes of investors and market participants.

My view is this: In theory, the notion of ''one market'' has a definite appeal from a variety of vantage points. The most powerful is that there are bound to be pricing relationships, dictated by mathematics, which bind together all of the segments of the equity markets—cash, futures, options.

But, in practice, we're a good distance from one market. These different markets have different trading mechanisms, have different counterparty risks, have different trading methodologies and styles, have different economic incentives for making markets, have different regulations, and have different customers.

So, while I wouldn't want to predict whether the future evolution of the system will produce one market, in the meantime we have to accept the reality: Imperfect linkages and the possibility of disruptive dynamics as the order imbalances in one market reverberate across other markets.

That underscores the need in our multimarket environment for better unification of regulatory approaches to related markets, so that the remaining limits on intermarket linkages are dealt with responsibly at the policy level.

Conclusion

I'm not discouraged by our economic prospects. U.S. industry has shown it can compete when basic currency prices and key economic variables are more or less in line. But with each and every year that goes by, the pressures of competition get greater. The bar gets raised higher. The costs of neglect of our physical plant or our human resources go higher. The failure to innovate, to improve product quality, to lower costs of production, and to use capital or human resources wisely brings stern penalties. For their part, government policymakers have to help get economic growth right down to the level of the business enterprise. That means a policy commitment to greater capital formation and a financial system capable of supporting the capital formation process.

Greater capital formation requires nurturing a stronger domestic savings flow to finance investment. We can't be dependent indefinitely on the savings of foreigners to finance our capital formation.

But greater capital formation is not a panacea for our economic growth problems. Just building more machines with better technology will still leave us short of our potential. And our full potential will never be reached without an educated, skilled work force whose innate creativity is given free rein.

Though more and more people pay lip service to the people side of the American economy, it is not being developed as well as it can be, and has to be. Many of our competitors abroad are doing a far better job. They will reap the benefit of greater flexibility in the workplace and, ultimately, higher productivity growth and enhanced competitiveness, much to our discomfort if we don't emulate them.

And we will not be able to emulate them if we continue to neglect the inadequacies of our education system, which is in trouble in many areas. For its part, American business has a long road to travel before it can legitimately claim to be in the international forefront of employee training and development.

Overcoming the education and training and development problems would still leave management with the tremendous job of reaping the benefits of workers' know-how; getting them to work more effectively and more cooperatively with one another as well as with management.

And as for the financial markets, we must not be lulled by recovery. We had better realize that there is a warning embodied in that market break: We can't take for granted our capacity to create earnings growth, to build better companies, and to be rewarded for it with higher stock values, if we don't do the things at the national and at the business enterprise level that will make us more productive. Otherwise, we have to face an unhappy future in a competitive world that will not excuse our mistakes and inadequacies.

The different financial markets are not insulated from one another. Each market is capable of sending shock waves which quickly reverberate in other markets. Measures must be carefully crafted to dissipate the shocks while preserving, and even enhancing, the unique functions of each of the markets.

The challenge to America as we prepare to compete in the world of tomorrow is to redo our physical capital, find better ways to nurture our people capital, and ensure that our financial markets are competitive and efficient.

This must be done because we are an increasingly entrepreneurial society in an increasingly entrepreneurial world. More people are taking risks because there are more rewards to be garnered.

The principle of risk and reward, like blue jeans and hamburgers, is an American export. But more so than physical goods, the blossoming of entrepreneurship promises a better way of life and provides hope for people. Not only is it a hope for people in the Western democracies, but it is a hope for those in the less-developed countries, and in Eastern Europe and China, and everywhere else. They're all beginning to use the same kinds of processes, the same kinds of products, and the same kinds of economic incentives.

In this new world economic environment, we must try to make ourselves more competitive so we can continue to raise this country's standard of living and create a better quality of life for every American. In the end, that is what competitiveness is all about.

Brief Summary: Question-and-Answer Session Following the Lecture

Q. As a co-chief executive officer of a New York Stock Exchange member firm, it has been a bit of a challenge to remain internationally competitive in the securities industry given the high cost of people capital in the seventies and eighties. Could you comment on the group of people in the securities industry who are earning an enormous amount of money for their companies and for themselves?

A. A good reason for that is that there has not been enough competition in some aspects of the business. I think that will correct itself over a period of time. In the more traditional lines of the securities business, the return on capital has been more in line with historical norms. There are problems today with the sales force and that will continue as long as firms are willing to pay ridiculous sums to lure salesmen from one another. Usually that comes and goes in cycles. Looking ahead, the industry probably will go through more consolidations. There will also be more entrants into the business, and more segmented competition. Profits will normalize over a period of time, because you are going to get more competition from other types of financial institutions.

London is a perfect example. Everybody moved in, spent a lot of money, and now some are moving out. There are a few firms that define their markets, execute that well, and make good money at it. But most firms there are suffering the consequences of too much money and too many people chasing too few products. As the rest of the world gets more competitive, returns are going to normalize and, perhaps, even be subnormal in some areas.

Furthermore, as the Japanese really get active in this market, there are going to be dramatic changes. They have the people and the capital. While they make people partners, they don't pay them what we pay them. Japanese workers work not just for themselves, they work for their company and they work for their country. In London, a lot of very young, bright Japanese people are paid about one-quarter of what Americans and Britons are paid there—and that's some kind of competition.

So, I think that the situation in our industry is going to normalize. We have to keep our costs down and get more productivity. We will have to find more efficient ways for firms to execute their orders, find better ways to provide liquidity and so forth. We've got to change like every other industry, and, hopefully, we will.

Q. You mentioned institutional trading and its effect on October 19, 1987. What do you see as the individual's role in capital investment if institutional trading can cause a reaction like that?

A. The strength of this market and why it has been so successful over the years is that it has allowed equal access to all people. Whether you want to buy 100 shares of IBM or a million shares, you can have simultaneous access to the pricing mechanism. I think that is a very, very important element to keep in the system. We have to resist segmenting the market, driving off individuals as well as institutions.

I don't know how significant individual participation will be in the future, but I do know that you must create an open and fair market to which everyone can have access. Many institutions, as professional as they are, act just like individuals. There are something like 13,000 institutions that use the Exchange in the course of a year, and two or three thousand that use it continually. Many of them enter the market on a random basis, much like individuals do. So, it is very, very important that you keep the market open and fair.

Q. What are you doing to prevent the computerized trading problem, and what are you doing with your member firms to prevent the problems that individuals have had in getting through to their brokers on October 19, 1987?

A. To take the second question first, at the NYSE we did a survey of individual investors and a small percentage of them had problems, but most of them didn't try to access the market. I think that on any day, if you have an account executive that has fifty accounts and all of them want to call him at once, there isn't much you are going to be able to do about that. We have been working with member firms to put in better communications facilities, but if suddenly everybody wants to communicate with a broker, you're always going to have some problems.

Computerized trading is another, and more difficult, matter. You can't do away with computers, you can't do away with modern communications. What you've really got to do is slow things down, so that everybody can get on the highway at the same time and be treated exactly the same way. We have tried to put what we call a collar on the market. This has to do with arbitrage between the futures market and the equities market. If stock prices fluctuate more than 50 points in any one day, either up or down, we take program trades off the system. For that and for a variety of other reasons, the market seems to have stabilized a little bit for the present.

The big question in the future, whether you have a

hundred shares or whether you're managing a billion hares, is what happens when you want to get out of everything at once and you press that button. We really haven't solved that problem except to say "stop!" or "slow down!" or "there is a queue here." The problems in October 1987 were caused basically by a dozen institutions. I said earlier that at least 2,000 institutions continually use our marketplace. But what happens if fifty—or a hundred—large institutions want to do the same thing at the same time? They can't do it. So, the market is going to adjust in some way to that.

Hopefully, institutions have learned their lessons from October 1987, but the problem is still something that we're very concerned about. You cannot provide instant liquidity anywhere in the world with the kind of demand for instant liquidity we had. Whether we can do it in five years or ten years is something else. It cannot be done now and if it happens again, you're going to get the same kind of dislocation.

Q. My theoretical question deals with the subject of your talk tonight, people. Colleges and universities turn out a lot of educated people and, hopefully, most of them are qualified to do what they do. But there is large gap in the trades and the lower-level skills. I have offices in New York and New Jersey and I can't get a secretary. It's a terrible problem. Schools obviously need help and the government is cutting aid to education. Where do you see the private economy going in aiding the private institutions? Not universities, but those schools and corporations that are educating people in the vocational, practical, and technical skills that business will need to grow?

A. Hopefully, we have tried to address that a little bit. First, I wouldn't want to let the universities off the hook. I really do wish that it were true that we are getting literate people who could think and write clearly, at least write a page and a half of something that makes some sense. Second, every business is in the business of training; it must be in the business of training. Hopefully, you don't have to train employees to read and write, you train them to do other things. I think that is part of the Japanese experience, the Tandem experience; that's part of the experience of every successful company.

The emphasis is not on the private school system because if this country is to survive and continue to be great, it must resuscitate its public school system. That depends on every citizen in every school district insisting that the schools produce well-educated students. But it also means that business must be willing to help in some way; providing jobs, providing some kinds of training until we get down the road to where our schools are producing the kinds of people who are adaptable to change. It is just an enormous problem, and nobody's got the right answer yet. You're asking the right question; I wish that we had the right answer.

I was just in Tucson, Arizona. There is something there called the Business and Higher Education Forum. In a recent three-day conference they covered the whole subject of what business can do and what schools can do. They had business and university people and they had foundation people, who were willing to put money into the process. There have been experiments like the Boston Compact—there are other similar experiments going on all over the place. But we still, right here in this city, cannot produce a public school system that can create an incentive for all the students to go through that system. Very difficult. I wish that I had the answer to it, but I don't. It's crucial to our survival.

Q. What is your outlook and comfort level regarding specialist capital?

A. There is not enough capital in any of the financial markets. It's one of the problems of the late eighties and nineties. How we get enough capital in the system—whether it be banking, the specialist system, or whatever else we're doing—is an extremely difficult problem. It concerns the proper functioning of the markets. Hopefully, some capital can be generated internally through earnings. As far as the specialist system is concerned, it normally has enough capital for its everyday function. But it doesn't have enough capital for a 500-point drop in the market in one day. We will soon increase the capital requirement for specialists and will require specialists to get large lines of credit from different banks. But admittedly, the problem with lines of credit is that they may not be there when you need them.

We have also changed our rules to enable broad line brokerage firms to own specialist units without restricting existing operations. The next step is to attract non-securities industry companies with reasonably deep pockets into the specialist business. So, I think that the specialist business is in a rapid transition. It definitely needs more capital, like everything else in the financial system, and I think that we are working actively to bring it in.

Q. What are your feelings on trading hours for the New York Stock Exchange?

A. I don't think that in the next couple of years there will be a change in trading hours. There just doesn't seem to be much pressure for it right now. We extended it to 9:30 and you really would have thought that we had revolutionized the world. Every time you mention trading hours, people begin to shake and shudder. I had a woman at a golf club stop me and say, what are you doing to my son-in-law, he's got two young children. I replied, my God, what happened to him. She said, well, he's got to be in there by 9:30 now. What *really* happens is that he has to be there two hours before opening, so he has to get in there by 7:30. I don't see much thrust now for an extension of trading hours. That might change again. You know, our industry changes rapidly and ideas change rapidly, but right now there seems to be no pressure for longer hours.

As regards 24-hour trading in connection with the globalized market, right now I think that a lot of people don't find it practical. There were a lot of lessons in October 1987—and the limitations of 24-hour trading may be one of them.